THE VIETNAM VETERANS MEMORIAL

THE VIETNAM VETERANS MEMORIAL

by
MICHAEL KATAKIS

Essay by
KRIS HARDIN, PH.D.

Foreword by
ROBERT KERREY

CROWN PUBLISHERS, INC.   NEW YORK

ACKNOWLEDGMENTS

My thanks to the following for their support, encouragement, straight talk, and invaluable counsel: Kris Hardin; Robert Kerrey; Leigh Wiener; Cary Porter; Evelyn Loewendahl; David Groff; Wilson Henley; Ivan and Patricia Karp; Gene Stratton; David V. Schlink; Jack Voorzanger; Nick Barnett; Linda Barnett; Maya Ying Lin; Ralph Starkweather; Dave Gardner; Leica U.S.A., Inc.; and my wife, for her unconditional love and support.

Published by Crown Publishers, Inc., 225 Park Avenue South, New York, New York 10003, and represented in Canada by the Canadian MANDA Group

CROWN is a trademark of Crown Publishers, Inc.

Manufactured in Japan

Library of Congress Cataloging-in-Publication Data

Katakis, Michael.
The Vietnam Veterans Memorial.
1. Vietnam Veterans Memorial (Washington, D.C.)—
Pictorial works.   I. Title.
DS559.83.W18K37   1988   959.704'38   88-7020

Book design by June Marie Bennett

ISBN 0-517-57019-X

10 9 8 7 6 5 4 3 2 1

First Edition

For my father,
George E. Katakis,
and in memory of my mother,
Catherine Katakis

FOREWORD

As I make the effort to remember Vietnam, the focus of my attention is on the present. Remembering the past should make life better, richer, more just, and more free.

When I remember, my conscience causes me to feel remorse for actions of mine that hurt other human beings or disappointed me. Unlike guilt, which can make it difficult to live and can even produce a paralysis of action, remorse helps me feel responsible for myself. Conscience-activated responsibility is like a light that illuminates possibilities I did not know were there.

When I remember, I recall again that freedom is the gift of yourself to someone else. Neither the voice of the cynic nor the cry of the pessimist can tarnish the memory of those on the wall who loved enough to give themselves to us.

When the philosopher William James, who hated war in all circumstances, said that he wished in peacetime for "the moral equivalency of war," he was observing this extraordinary capacity for sacrifice. When we fear losing everything, we are slaves. When we fear losing nothing, we are free.

It is my hope and sincere wish that our collective effort to remember will enable us to build a more complete self and a better world.

The political lessons learned from Vietnam are less important to me than the simple observations of those who fought there. Jim Garrett, a Lakota Sioux, whose homeland is in South Dakota, said that the war taught him that this world's community is much larger than he had imagined. The Vietnamese, he said, were more like him than he had expected a foreign people to be.

Gary Parrott said that if there is reincarnation, he hopes to return as a Vietnamese. He admires their strength of family, community, and history.

These are lessons learned from looking outside ourselves and seeing something more valuable than even our own lives. It is a recognition which gives us great power and potential. We dare not squander it.

The pictures in this book stir us to recall events long since forgotten. Do not lament this rekindling of old passions. Be grateful for the mysteries of life and the special understanding we have of it. It is a secret we have an obligation to tell.

Robert Kerrey
Omaha, Nebraska

PREFACE

When people come to the Vietnam Veterans Memorial they look for names, and in the reflection of the granite they see themselves. They remember, grieve, say good-bye, and sometimes heal. I have photographed many of these people at a critical point in their lives. In my two years of photographing the memorial I've seen thousands of faces and heard hundreds of stories and all have been deeply moving.

Not too long ago I was at the memorial. It was early morning. The sky was dull gray; the light soft and dim. The rain the night before had left the air heavy with moisture. As I had done so many times over the years, I began to walk up and down the memorial and look at the different things that had been left there the day before. There was a bottle of beer with a note attached, a POW bracelet, assorted flowers, American flags, a Purple Heart, two Bronze Stars, and a love letter from a sweetheart to her deceased fiancé. As I continued along the east wall, I came upon a pole stuck in the ground. It was about four feet high, and at the bottom was a small sign that read: ONLY ONE SON. Above the sign was a picture of a handsome young man in uniform, and around the photograph were small delicate flowers placed lovingly in perfect order. Above the picture was a medal from Vietnam and the young man's name. Above that was a medal of Jesus. Finally, at the top of the pole were Greek and American flags. I began to photograph this tribute, and as I was working someone tapped me on the shoulder.

Without looking up, I said, "Yes?"

A man with a heavy accent asked, "Do you like this?"

Again without looking up, I said, "How could anyone not like this? It was done with a lot of love."

"This is my son," the man said.

I stood and saw a gray-haired man in a dark suit in his late sixties or seventies, his eyes filled with tears. I reached for his hand and said, "I'm sorry. I'm so very sorry."

The man began to tell me about his son and why he had felt it his duty to serve in Vietnam. He reached into his coat pocket and pulled out a stack of photographs of his son's grave in Wisconsin. Next to the grave in most of the photographs was the mother of the boy. She wore black. The man told me that she had worn black for the last ten years.

The day went on and I continued to work; the man was there all day. He would talk to people who looked like veterans, and he'd ask if they had known his son. After thirteen hours I left. The man was still there.

Later that night I remembered my first visit to the memorial. I had gone to pay my respects to a boy I had known in high school, and I had been completely unprepared for my reaction when I saw his name. I remembered how that experience had led me to want to photograph the tragedy of war and its legacy. I wanted to do much more than just photograph the people and situations around the memorial. I wanted to understand them as well. After thinking further, I realized that for a long time my work had perhaps veered away from this direction. Instead of focusing on historical context, it had come to focus on individual lives. There were no answers in my photographs, no deep intellectual analyses that gave new insights or profound conclusions, no eloquent tributes. Just images of people left behind to deal with the past. I remember being disappointed. In the end, though, now that the last shutter has clicked and the book is finished, I do not feel so far from my original goal. The legacy of war that has so often been invisible does have to do with the people left behind, their lives, and how they move on. From this vantage point, as these photographs show, it is the living who haunt us as much as the dead.

Three perspectives, I felt, were necessary to complete this work: the words of someone who served in Vietnam, of someone who has watched others deal with their loss, and of someone who lost a friend. The former governor of Nebraska, Robert Kerrey, recipient of the Medal of Honor for his service in Vietnam, has graciously contributed some of his personal reflections. Dr. Kris Hardin, a sociocultural anthropologist at the University of Pennsylvania, offers her insights into the Vietnam era and the history of the Vietnam Veterans Memorial. And finally, I share with you the story of a young man who lived and died.

Michael Katakis

GHOSTS IN THE WALL

I am one of the lucky ones. I have no names to look up in the books that line the walkways as you enter the Vietnam Veterans Memorial. Instead, I have fading memories of an era—news clips of battle scenes, protest marches, atrocities; stories of political intrigue; a growing sense of frustration as the conflict wore on; and a sense of relief when the American troops came home.

As a rule, war memorials do not celebrate memories like mine. We are used to images of victorious soldiers frozen in time, like the Iwo Jima Memorial, or of generals on horseback. But there were too many contradictions and divided loyalties about our presence in Vietnam to allow us to glorify in conventional ways those who fought there. To the American public and to many of the soldiers who fought it, the war was a relentless grind with no major victories, no turning points to commemorate, no obvious heroes. Nightly newscasts during the conflict made the activities of war so accessible that for the first time we were brought face to face with the sight of war. Often our reactions to the horror were so overwhelming that we lost sight of the men and women who were just doing their jobs.

By the end of the Vietnam conflict, it was clear that America was a nation of fragmented loyalties. We had loyalties to those who had served when asked, to moral issues, to a country, to a political system, and to a way of life. As a result, many soldiers returned to find themselves caught in a kind of cross fire. I still remember stories of veterans being spat on when they finally reached their hometown airports. For the first time in American history, those who survived a war arrived home to fight a new war. They were blamed for even being in Vietnam; they were subtly blamed for reminding us that we, as Americans, had been unable to accomplish what we set out to do. The criticism, neglect, and abuse of veterans as they returned was only one indication of the tensions we faced as a nation, and how hard it would be for us to resolve those tensions in the future.

Men returning from other wars have been treated differently. At the end of World War II soldiers returned in large groups. When they reached the United States they were met by welcoming parades, a government that was proud of them, a government and citizenry who accepted responsibility for their actions in a time of war. Whatever the soldiers had been compelled to do was characterized as a necessary act of a necessary war; thus it was accepted and forgotten. The soldiers were presented as heroes on a grand scale, with all the gratitude and public recognition that that implies. Equally important, those who had waited at home were assured—through the actions of government, their fellow citizens, and the media—that their loved ones had performed a valued and honorable service for their country and for humankind.

Contrast World War II with Vietnam. In the 1960s young men were drafted for a period of two years, one of which was usually spent in Vietnam. Soldiers were constantly returning throughout the conflict; they did not all come back at once as they had in 1945. When they returned from Vietnam, they were rapidly and silently scattered. There were no victory parades, no recognition of service. We had no images other than those of tired, often disheartened individuals who returned and then disappeared, taking with them the confusion they represented.

The way in which the veterans came back after Vietnam is also important. When the veterans of World War II returned, it took most of them several weeks or even months to reach their homes. During this time they were with other veterans, men or women with experiences similar to their own. There was time to discuss, to reminisce, to find out that others also had had to make difficult moral choices, to be reassured that they were not alone and that others had shared their horrors. When a soldier's tour of duty was up in Vietnam, he was brought home as quickly as possible. With the speed of travel today there was little opportunity to compare experiences with others, little chance to realize others had lived through the same kinds of nightmares and been forced to make similar kinds of choices. There was little time to heal. This was especially critical because in Vietnam, we were suddenly faced with an uncertain enemy. Our soldiers fought not only troops like themselves, but for the first time women, the elderly, and even children.

Is it any wonder the returnees often had trouble fitting immediately back into the lives they had left several years before? Writer Joel Swerdlow described the experiences of returning veterans in this way:

> After twelve months they were put on an air-conditioned airplane with pretty stewardesses, and suddenly the war was over. "Wash up," one returning veteran's mother had said. "Your welcome-home dinner is ready." He looked down at his hands. Mud from Vietnam was still under his fingernails.*

Many of the veterans with whom photographer Michael Katakis spoke at the Vietnam Veterans Memorial had similar experiences, feelings of having gone through something that had altered their lives or changed the kind of people they were. They speak of not being able to describe, examine, or understand those changes, and of having found few people around them willing to listen. One veteran, who asked that his name not be used, wrote about it this way:

> They say you can never go home again. I returned from Vietnam looking exactly like the boy who had left; everyone (even I) thought they were

*Swerdlow, Joel. 1985. "To Heal a Nation." *National Geographic*, Vol. 167, #5: p. 554.

getting the same boy back. No one wanted that more than I. But the boy had changed and we all resented him for that.

I look in the mirror and I see his face. I live in his body. I live in his home. I savor all his memories and protect all his secrets as if they were my own. I love all the people who once loved him. I exist in the life that should have been his, but I'm not him. I lost his soul and we all hate me for that.

Many of the veterans photographed for this book talked about the changes they felt upon their return and the difficulties of forgetting what they had been through in Vietnam and fitting in again at home.

As the veterans drifted back, their relatives and friends became responsible for integrating them into society and dealing with the changes that many of the veterans themselves found difficult to characterize. Many of these friends and relatives were simply unprepared for this burden. Part of the problem was that we had only a limited understanding of what had really gone on in Vietnam. Perhaps there was reticence on our part to know more; perhaps there was reticence on the part of the veterans to relive their experiences.

While those of us who stayed home may have been painfully aware of the moral decisions all servicemen are forced to make, our government (and we as its citizens) was unwilling to accept responsibility for those decisions. As a result we found ourselves faced with unanswered questions. Could there be heroes in a war that was still going on and that we seemed to be losing? Could you fight in an unjust conflict and still be a noble person? Could you serve in Vietnam and not be involved in the kinds of atrocities reported by the press? Is there value in doing what your government asks, even if you don't agree or even if those at home seem overwhelmingly opposed to it? These questions and many others went unanswered.

The easiest way for the veterans, their families, and friends to cope was to ignore those questions and try to move on from where relationships had left off several years earlier, to disregard the contradictions in the hopes that time and subsequent experiences would make them less important.

In the midst of our confusion about how to treat the returning veterans, the families of those who lost someone in Vietnam were even more isolated. This was not the conscious decision of a callous society but more a result of our inability to resolve the contradictions we faced. While there were certainly ceremonies at Arlington National Cemetery for some, or special burials in local cemeteries by ministers and veterans' groups for others, most of these deaths remained individual sacrifices. There was no national recognition for what many veterans call "the ultimate sacrifice," and from this rose a growing sense that those who were dying were giving their lives for a lost cause. "It is so hard to give a son, especially to the lost cause which was Vietnam," wrote one father.

Families such as these were caught between two poles—believing that when the country asks you to serve there is no question of what you must do, but feeling also that the Vietnam conflict was unjust. For those who lost sons or daughters, grief could only be compounded by the unanswered questions. As the photographs and statements here show, some have moved on. Others have been unable to move past their tragedy and will carry a debilitating grief with them for the rest of their lives.

Slowly, over the last fifteen years, we have revised our images of Vietnam and its veterans and have begun to answer some of our questions. It doesn't really matter if we have the "correct" answers. What is important is that the questions and answers are shared. The healing process has begun to move from the personal and the individual toward a kind of national understanding. This consensus is not in the guise of government programs or government recognition, but in the form of individuals making their own evaluations of the era, reaching similar conclusions, and acting upon them. The building of the Vietnam Veterans Memorial is only one of these actions. Perhaps it is the most important statement about those who served in Vietnam, but it is connected to many smaller gestures that have also tried to answer our questions.

We have not yet reached the end of the questions, but we have reached the point of recognizing that we put the Vietnam veterans in an impossible situation. Perhaps we are able to see this now because time has made the contradictions less sharp. Maybe we have become uncomfortably aware that what we hoped would disappear has only festered with time and that our images of Vietnam do not really mesh with reality. At any rate, a kind of consensus has begun to take shape as ideas are shared and reshaped, a process that only happens over time in any society. It happened as the same kinds of questions and ideas surfaced repeatedly and spontaneously in countless ordinary places, at countless ordinary times, in the lives of countless individuals. It happened as veterans made the American public more aware of the Vietnam conflict through legal disputes connected with Agent Orange and veterans' benefits, and through the possibility of finding POWs and MIAs still alive. It is not that these conversations and events changed our notions of the Vietnam era, but more that through them it became increasingly apparent that we could not yet rest.

Changing media images of Vietnam, particularly the changing issues on which films about the war and its veterans have focused, have also helped in our re-evaluation of the Vietnam era. *Apocalypse Now,* one of the first films about the war, depicted Vietnam almost as a fantasy. *Coming Home,* a later film, went further by presenting the American public with graphic images of the problems faced by returning veterans. *The Deer Hunter* combined this with vivid images of real life in Vietnam. But it was not until movies such as *Platoon* that the Vietnam War films began to really consider questions of right and wrong. This brought back to the forefront the same questions with which we had been wrestling for more than a decade. We still have few answers, but at least it is becoming all right, maybe even required, that such questions be asked.

Given this context, it is difficult to imagine a memorial that uses a single battle or hero to remind us of our presence in Vietnam or to represent and honor those who fought. Rather, we chose at last to honor—in a very personal way—those who served and to memorialize those men and women who died or are missing in action.

The memorial is a list of names. Etched on black granite walls are the names of the men and women who died or are still missing. The monument and people's reactions to it make little reference to the divisions that grew during the war. There are no designations of heroes here, no signs of atrocity, no signs of victory or defeat. Some of their names are marked by crosses to show those who are missing in action, but these marks do not distinguish draftees from volunteers, commitment from malaise, or all the shades in between. What we have done is to present our loss in a way that invites friends and relatives to ponder the names and memories of their loved ones in a setting that makes only slight reference to the larger questions—how and why they died, and whether it was right or wrong.

Instead, it is the names themselves we find so compelling. In numbers they show the extent of our loss. They allow the living and the dead to come together, bound by memories and speculation about what might have been. The names provide a focus for the memorial, a focus that the actual events of the conflict and our larger questions cannot provide.

Nearly fifteen years after our complete withdrawal from South Vietnam, Americans are still trying to come to terms with the contradictions that plagued our presence there. The best any society can hope for in such circumstances is to somehow work out a kind of understanding about what has happened.

Reaching such a consensus is never easy. For us it is a long and painful task. One reason it has taken so long stems from the fact that it has been such a highly personal endeavor until recently. By calling it a personal task, I mean that we, as individuals (whether veterans, parents of veterans, or friends of those who served), were required for the first time in American history to construct our own images of what had happened in a conflict and to develop our own ways of integrating the veterans back into American society.

From its conception, the memorial has helped to crystallize our attitudes toward the Vietnam era and its veterans. Controversies that erupted during the course of its building mirror the questions we have been trying to resolve for the past fifteen years. Completion of the memorial, despite these controversies, reflects our ability to reach a certain kind of consensus. We know a little better now how we feel about Vietnam—about those who fought and died there and those who fought and survived.

From the very beginning the memorial was a grass-roots project, sponsored and funded by individuals rather than the American government. The idea for the memorial may have occurred to many veterans, but when it hit Jan Scruggs after seeing *The Deer Hunter*, he decided to do something about it. In 1979 Scruggs announced his plans to build a memorial to those who had served in Vietnam. It would be paid for from donations rather than government funds, it would make no political statements, and it would list the names of all those who had died in the Vietnam conflict.

While some suggested the best place for the memorial was Arlington National Cemetery, the organizers felt it would be more appropriate to have it inside the capital, instead of across the Potomac. Allocating land inside the capital would at last signal to the veterans that the nation had recognized the sacrifices made for their country. The organizers also felt that having the memorial in Arlington National Cemetery was problematic because they wanted to do more than just honor the dead. After much lobbying, all one hundred senators finally sponsored a bill to allow the memorial to be built on a grassy space between the Lincoln and Washington memorials. President Jimmy Carter signed the bill into law in early July 1980, a little more than a year after Jan Scruggs announced plans for the memorial.

Once the location was decided upon, a national design competition was held. Designs from all over the country were submitted, some from professional artists, some from veterans, some from ordinary citizens—1,421 entries in all. They were judged by a panel of internationally known architects, designers, and critics. There were few rules in the competition. Entrants had to meet four guidelines: designs had to be reflective and contemplative in character; they had to fit in with the neighboring monuments; they had to contain all the names of those who died or were still missing; and they could make no political statements about the war.

A winning design was selected and presented to the organizing committee, and then the uproar began. While some disagreed with the idea of a memorial at all, the major dispute centered around what the memorial should say about the veterans, about America, and about the Vietnam War. The nature of this dispute is hardly surprising given the complicated feelings most Americans had about the war and those who fought.

Maya Ying Lin, the winner of the competition, described her entry in this way:

> Many earlier war memorials were propagandized statements about the victor, the issues, the politics, and not about the people who served and died. I felt a memorial should be honest about the reality of war and be for the people who gave their lives. . . . I didn't want a static object that people would just look at, but something they could relate to as on a journey, or passage, that would bring each to his own conclusions. . . . I wanted to work with the land and not dominate it. I had an impulse to cut open the earth . . . an initial violence that in time would heal. The grass would grow back, but the cut would remain, a pure, flat surface, like a geode when you cut into it and polish the edge. I didn't visualize heavy physical objects implanted in the earth; instead it was as if the black-brown earth were polished and made into an interface between the sunny world and the quiet, dark world beyond, that we can't enter.*

Although Maya Ying Lin won the competition when she was only twenty, it was clear from the beginning that the organizing committee was dealing with a professional. Although others seemed to be having trouble visualizing the design, she knew exactly how it

*Lin, Maya Ying. 1985. "America Remembers." *National Geographic*, Vol. 167, #5: p. 557.

would look and what effect it would have on people. When Michael Katakis and I spoke with her, she told of reading about how people deal with grief in different places around the world in order to understand it, and of knowing that the memorial would be a place where people would weep. She kept much of this vision to herself during the planning and construction of the memorial, feeling that if others knew the extent of the emotions her work would produce, they might withdraw their support of her design, even though it had the backing of the judges.

There were some who opposed her plan. In testimony before the Fine Arts Commission of Washington, the proposed wall was described as a "black gash of shame" that presented service in Vietnam in a negative light. The organizers of the memorial were divided in opinion, some supporting the original design, others wanting to alter the design to make it appear more patriotic.

When she talks about the opposition to her design now, Lin sees things in political terms. She intentionally focused on the names of the dead and left out sculptural depictions of battles and valor; she wanted to present the dead as individuals, something she feels the military is reluctant to recognize. She speaks of military training as a melding of separate people into larger groups that can survive only because a degree of individuality is lost. In her opinion, soldiers cannot be seen as individuals when they fight or when they die. Generals or those in charge would be unable to go on if they saw their soldiers as anything other than replaceable parts.

Initially, controversy over the design aided fund-raisers because it brought attention to plans for the memorial. During this time donations for the monument were being solicited from corporations, veterans' groups, unions, church groups, defense contractors, and most importantly from private individuals. Along with the money contributed by individuals, thousands of letters and notes were sent, describing for whom the money was donated and revealing personal stories of grief. With each note it became more and more apparent how important it was for people to have somewhere to voice these stories. It became clear that telling the stories and listening to those told by others allowed people to share important parts of their lives, to realize others had lived through many of the same experiences, and to see that many people were asking the same kinds of questions.

Finally, the controversy about the design was settled with a compromise—the wall would stay, but a statue and flag would be added. After further arguments it was decided the statue and flag would be placed to one side and the integrity of the original design would be maintained.

Today people come to the memorial from all walks of life to search out the names of those they knew. In this process they confront the past and the possibilities of what might have been—for those who have died, as well as for themselves. A woman from the Midwest leaves letters to her fiancé saying she'll never love another and that she misses him. A stepfather lifts a boy on his shoulders so he can touch his father's name. A man leaves a pair of combat boots for his brother with an American flag stuffed inside. A five-year-old asks his father, "Did all these people really die?" Someone leaves a bottle of beer for a pal. A veteran remembers that Vietnam was the best part of his life, except for the dying.

Through these gestures we are able to see those who died or are missing as individuals—real people with real histories. They were friends, lovers, husbands, wives, children, parents. Letters to loved ones, photographs of a prom night long ago, mementos of the war, and especially the tears allow us to see the immensity of the loss and to consider the meaning of morality, the extent of our commitment to freedom and country, and myriad other thoughts and emotions.

These photographs demonstrate that the living can haunt us as much as the dead. Many of the visitors to the wall are torn between loyalty to those who served their country and loyalty to moral issues. Some of these images are of people unable to move forward; others are of people in transition. All show the personal costs of war, regardless of politics. In this open, communal setting the extent of our loss—in terms of those who have died as well as those who live on—is made visible.

Kris Hardin

Many thanks to Sandie Fauriol, Ivan Karp, Michael Katakis, and Maya Ying Lin for discussing parts of this essay with me.

THE VIETNAM VETERANS MEMORIAL

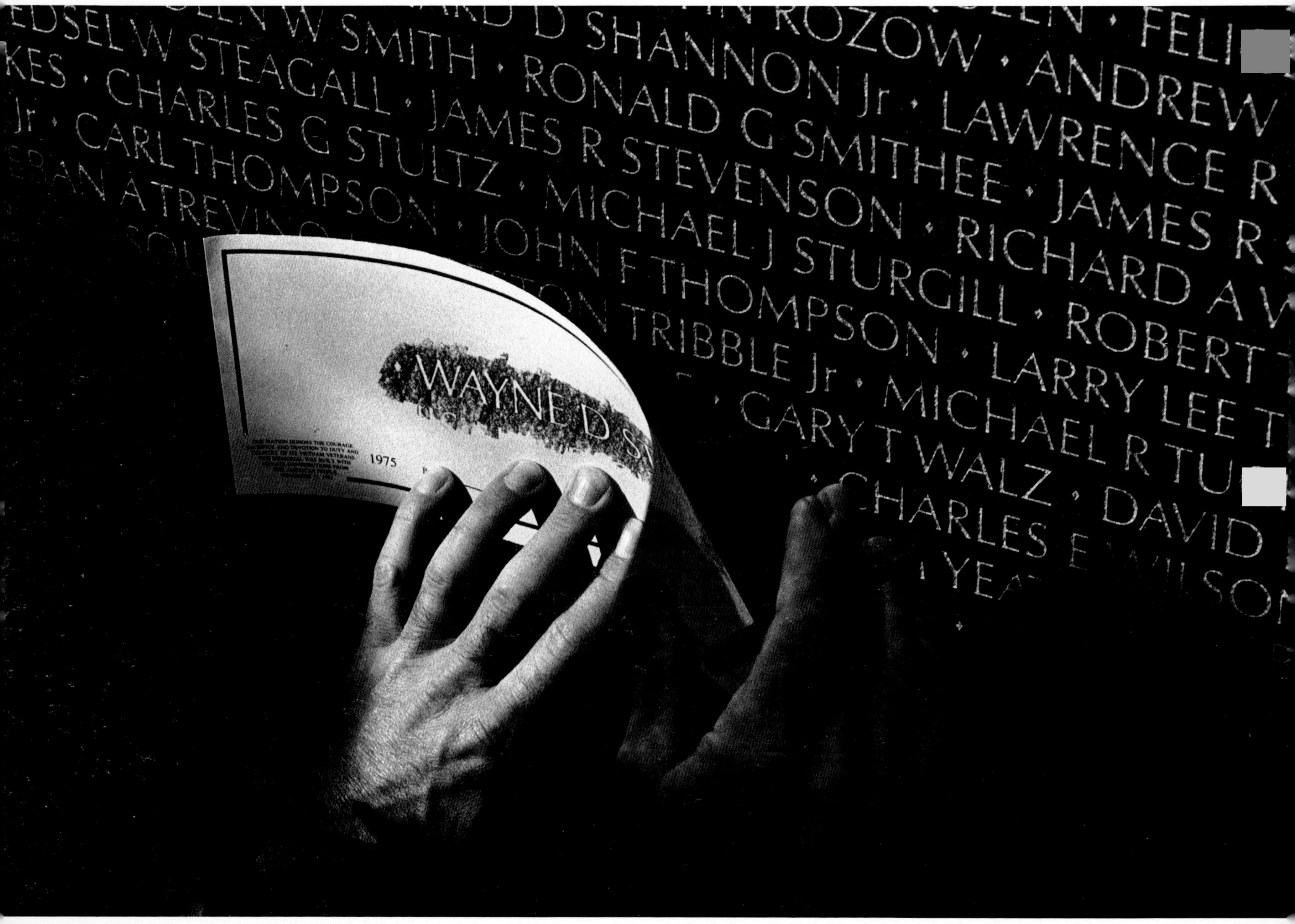

WALL 25, LINE 91

In Washington, at the Vietnam Veterans Memorial, I made my way to the books that hold all the names of the dead. As I turned the pages, I remembered him as he was and hoped somehow that his name wasn't there, knowing of course that it was, and finding it. Wayne Douglas Stigen, Chicago: W25, L91.

The Washington Monument and the Capitol were directly in front of me as I walked along the narrow stone path next to the wall and its thousands of names. A man in his thirties stood in front of the wall, staring, a small boy at his side. They held hands and after a moment the boy looked up and asked, "Daddy, why do people go to war if they know they're going to die?" The man looked at the child and smiled sadly.

I didn't cry when I heard about Wayne's death. I think I just got angry, then numb, and finally silent. As I walked past the endless names, searching for Wall 25, I was numb and silent, the same feeling I had had twenty years earlier.

At Wall 25, I began looking for Line 91. The black granite reflected my image and I clearly saw my face; then there he was. I stared for a moment, not at the name but at my reflection. I had changed; my hair had some gray and the lines around my eyes showed experience and wear. I reached out to touch his name and felt my friend was the same, still eighteen. Young people who die are frozen forever in time. Everything around the names would change in time. The people who would come year after year would see their reflections in the stone, their hair would gray, their bodies age. They would change, but all these names would remain as they were, forever.

I touched Wayne's name and began to cry. I cried for a long time, and the granite reflected my sadness and release. I was finally able to say good-bye to my friend. I knew he would always be here.

Michael Katakis

The Vietnam War has damaged me for life, forever.
I don't think it was a fair war.
I believe if it had been a declared war
a lot of our young sons would be home today.
God bless you, America.
Our sons fought and died for you.

―――

Evelyn Barbour
Richmond, Virginia

Time does not heal all wounds.
I'll never let anyone forget.
I saw man's inhumanity to man, ours and theirs.
Where is victory? What is defeat?

———

D. F. Didyoung
Reading, Pennsylvania

Vietnam was not just another war
and the Vietnam Memorial is not just another wall.
Only when we recognize that each represents
an integral part of our lives
can the healing process begin.

———

Bill Struck
Arnold, Maryland

They go away feeling more
at peace with themselves.

———

Lee Adriani
Volunteer, Vietnam Veterans Memorial
Camp Springs, Maryland

I would go again to help people
who love freedom as we do.

———

Dick E. Ellis
Arlington, Virginia

If I make one person realize that Vietnam was hell,
then I have done my job.
I will always thank those who gave,
but I'll never forget what we lost.

———

Bill Struck
Arnold, Maryland

We did everything they asked us to,
and we have no apologies to make for anything.

―――――

James Heckman
Osceola, Indiana

I buried the dead in Vietnam;
that was my job.
I'm tired of burying the dead.

―――――

Anonymous

We should never allow a political leader
to plunge us into a political war again.
These boys died like it was a real war,
but it wasn't.

―――――

Jack Berry
Charlotte, North Carolina

If they gave me back my legs I'd go back again.

Chuck Eatley
Virginia

It makes you seem so small that so many
gave their most precious gift: life.

Daniel B. Harvey
Atlanta, Georgia

29

A part of me died over there,
and deep inside I will never be the same.

———

William Kenealy
Baltimore, Maryland

*Don't volunteer to fight
in a conflict you can't win,
or your war will never end.*

———

Joe Ropel
Somerdale, New Jersey

Jimmy had a feeling he would not come back.
I knew he would not.
He had a long talk with me and his dad.
He told me that the world did not hold
a mother that could be better to her sons.
He said he loved me with all his heart.
He said, "Mom, I am all right with the man up there."
He pointed to the sky.
He died August 27, 1968, and
in thirteen days his body came home.

———

Evelyn Barbour
Richmond, Virginia

*Our backs are against the wall and our job
is not done until everybody is home.*

———

Gary Barnes
Woodstock, New York

He was in the open in a rice paddy,
and a sniper shot him dead.
The sun came up nice that day.
It was beautiful.

———

Jackson Gibson
Thoreau, New Mexico

Where were you?

———

Vince Rios
San Francisco, California

There are moments when in my meditations
he still comes to me, and we talk.

———

Daniel Sabia
Los Angeles, California

Rich kids didn't go to Vietnam.
I felt good about what I was doing in 1965.
I became disillusioned in 1968.
They turned it into a meat grinder.

———

James A. Thompson

I blame the people of this country
for the suicides of Vietnam veterans.

———

Ben Fontana
Chicago, Illinois

Why did it have to happen? What was it for?
When I came home it was not the place I had left.
I was lost in my own country.

———

Gary Wright
Northern Virginia

47

My cousin never saw his baby.
He went over while his wife was pregnant—
we never saw him after that.

———

David Stafford
Maryland

50

Our son and only son was a Greek-American hero
who fought in an American war.
He will be remembered in our hearts
for the rest of our lives.

———

Tanos Kokalis
South Milwaukee, Wisconsin

Freedom is not free;
it comes on the installment plan.
If you don't pay the price,
they take it away.

———

Mike Gaddy
Asheville, North Carolina

The memorial puts you in the Vietnam War.
You see the names, but you see yourself, too,
and that makes you part of it.

———

Jerry Denney
Washington, D.C.

JAMES JOHNSON Jr · MARION E MEE · TERRENCE P O'BOYLE
DENNIS H DALE · ARTHUR FISHER
JAMES C WASHINGTON Jr
FRANCIS A ZERGGEN · DENNIS L ZIEBARTH · JAMES I BOWDREN Jr
JIMMY RAY CALLISON · JOHN R MUCCI · RICHARD C SCHOENBERG
BRENT A HAYTON · ROBERT L HUDSON · MATEO JUAREZ
RONALD D LE FEBURE · MICHAEL T MARTIN · ROGER L RITSCHARD
DARRELL B RICKER · ROBERT C RUNGE · ELISHA R SAINT CLAIR
MARTIN I ARBEIT · DAVID A BRYAN · VICTOR L ELLINGER
MICHAEL D GEHRT · ROBERT C GOTTIER · PAUL G KELLEY
NORMAN F PALEY · ROBERT D PERRY · SAMUEL R SAITO
CHARLES R HAMILTON · MICHAEL N HUGHES · FREDDIE L LOCKHART
SAMUEL L GANTT · EDWARD D BURKETT · RALPH HOWELL
WILLIAM CIP ARIAS Jr · MARVIN S ARTHINGTON · ROBERT L BAKER
GOSZEWSKI · PAUL T GILLASPIE · JORGE L JOURDAN-FONT
FREDERICK M RADER III · MACARIO SANCHEZ Jr · DAVID C JAUREGUI
ALBERT HALL · FRANKLIN U BRECKENRIDGE · ROBERT J KOLY
RONALD E SMITH · EARNEST WILLIAMS
JOSEPH C BLACK
SAMUEL A GRAYS · CAUDILL II
JAMES F SAXBY · GREEN
ROBERT B JOHNSON
CECIL G MOYER · GRAYSON H NEWBERRY
JOSEPH A JACQUES · ROBERT D SCHNEIDER
ROBERT E YOUNG · E BAKER · ROBERT A BOJANEK
RAFAEL A DIAZ · FREDERICK L FIELD
JAMES D JONES · MOORE · JOHN C STRINGER II
FELIPE MORALES
LAVERNE D COYLE · KENNETH E CRAYNE · THOMAS W FRECH
WALTER D LAMBERT · JOE M PALACIO
L STALLINGS · JESUS M BERRIOS-RIVERA
FRANCISCO VEGA · JOHNNY P GARCIA
ROBERT L KING · SCOTT L SCHMIDT · JERRY D WALKER
HENRY L CHAVIS
KERMIT L MATTHEWS · HOWARD J SCOVILLE
RANDY D RAY
J SCHMERBECK · STEVEN C WILLIS
BILLIE R STROHL · ROBERT W TOLER Jr

I didn't know he was dead.
I had a feeling he might be.
I keep thinking of him as a gung-ho private.

———

Patricia Pavlin
New Jersey

The actual moment that I became
a conscientious objector was when I was confronted by
a pop-up target in the form of a Vietnamese woman.
What followed was a long period of trouble
and finally a bad discharge that was later reversed.
During this period the Vietnam combat veterans
who I met showed me every kindness.
They knew why I did not want to go.

———

Keith Keller
Los Angeles, California

I can't understand why it's taken so long
for the government to do something like this
for their families.

———

Kevin Lovell
Hendersonville, North Carolina

I think of all the things that have happened
since his death—marriage, career, gray hair, paunches—
and I wonder how these things would have affected him.
That's why it's so vital for me to find the men
in his company and his platoon who remember him,
and especially those who were with him that night,
all those days ago.

———

Daniel Sabia
Los Angeles, California

*I promise you this, that I will never
give up the struggle, never let your memory of sacrifice
be forgotten, and if God wills it,
I will see you again, in a place free from
human frailty and corruption.*

———

D. F. Didyoung
Reading, Pennsylvania

To all our Vietnam vets.
You were young, you did a good job.
We love you and are very proud of you.
———

Evelyn Barbour
Richmond, Virginia

Thanks to Maya Lin, Jan Scruggs, Frederic Hart,
and the American people who put up the memorial.
Thank you for the welcome home.
———

Edward Azevedo
Washington, D.C.

In reality I've never left the wall
or my friends. Miles cannot diminish
what Vietnam has begun in our lives.
The wall is only a reflection
of what holds us together.

―――

Jim Heckman
Indiana

I think it's one of the most
reverential places I've ever been.
It never lets you out.

―――

Karen Hardison
Virginia

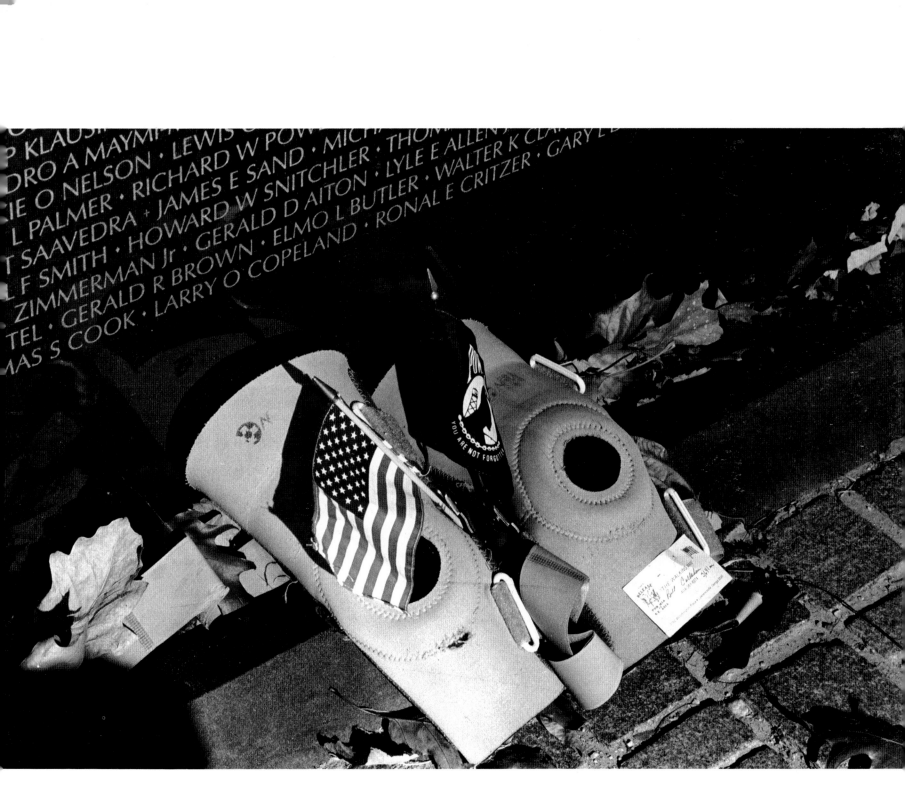

These were dedicated servicemen and -women
who went to Vietnam for love of country—
never realizing they would be so
unappreciated for so many years.

———

Gertrude Gerber
Maryland

Vietnam was a jungle, a gray quagmire
of politics and moral choices.
I honor the bravery of the men who fought there.
I ask that it be recognized that
courage comes in many forms.

Keith Keller
Los Angeles, California

LIST OF ILLUSTRATIONS